CREATEBITCOIN (CBTC)

create.davidgomadza7628102createbitcoin.start

www.createbitcoin.world

Whitepaper

DAVID GOMADZA

Copyright © 2024 David Gomadza

All rights reserved.

ISBN: 9798341308169

DEDICATION

A Better Future

CONTENTS

CREATEBITCOIN CBTC   1

MONEY PAPER IN CREATE CODE   9

ACKNOWLEDGMENTS

Tomorrow's World Order

CREATEBITCOIN CBTC

CREATEBITCOIN Whitepaper
05 October 2024 @ 10.18 UK time

Bitcoin in create code
create. .start
ax284861780
axt18786823864
atu184678386
aju143678901
apu2867890
aju2867890
atq267890
aou173867890
asa78980283
ajx18767890
aatuv18983867890
aao1838624184
aautr1867890
auttr167890386
arost18762984
ajut1848386
aqt67890386

abu7867890
aot193867890
aqt18367890
amnot1867890
aju2867890
ajv3867890
aux7890386
asut3867890
ajmn1828487890
ajq2867890
aajt187890
ajjut3867890
avtur867890
aat67890386
aaur6869038486
asur386789
apt285678
aot386780
aato39680
ajt286890
aut389024
asat267890
asao248678
aatr867890
autr983867
aoutr89284678
auty67890386
aatao67890284
ajur873892
avut867890386
aqar6798382
aumn8928678
axtr2867890
ajmn867890
aqur867890
aopt2867890
ajy287386

auy67890
aqmn867890
aarto28767890
aapt287283
aotur867890
autr3867890
amnop28486780
auy867890
ausart867890
aagm867890
aqr86283867890
argm28790
aaut392867890
aptmn67284386
aagr285386
aoutr2890386
aout2867890
aavutr867890
aat8490284
aat317890
agt28528678
aoutr28786
aumn867890284
aagt867890
aavg1890386
aouq867890
aompt867890
auyo1846718
aaxtu867890
aaxtu867890
avyo867823678
aourty867890
axxr867890
aagur184867890
ajaru867890
au28498
aq8678

aapo27890
aa286380
aa184286
at19286
aq7878680
ajyo86780
auyo8789283
aautr8678
aautr2178
aonm867890
ajqur28678
aerotq6670
axer67890
aaxr7898
axz286890
aj428678380
ajj7863828
ajjx77284

create.davidgomadza7628102bitcoinincreatecode.start

total supply 3867890286780
current value of 1 is $8

anything in create code cannot lose value instead with his longevity plans it gains in value
these are the equations
if we start issuing bitcoin in create code these are the starting values if we are to ask what can be bitcoin exactly in create code then what is the answer it is create.davidgomadza7628102createbitcoin.start

now our equations if bitcoin is in create code are
867890284890 was the starting value and now the current quantity is
3867890286780 and we start selling at US$8 from today 05 October 2024 at 10.18am now what this means is that we can start selling using the decree system where people buy and not give us money

at first as promise to pay us as price rises so here are our maximum bitcoin decrees we can give and hold we can if we accept decrees then what could be the effect this is the answer we ca tell everyone what createbitcoin is through a whitepaper

CREATEBITCOIN whitepaper

if we ask what createbitcoin is this is the answer the most clever way to represent real bitcoin in life without infringing on any rights because this is a different version that can stand in its own hence a new invention now if we say what can be createbitcoin then this is the answer it is real bitcoin but in create code that is handed out as decrees and when value reach 1 to US$8 we can start selling and asking for real money and as it matches bitcoin we can calculate the value based on the true value in such a way that we have the true bitcoin in create code at the end through assimilation and if we ask what can be createbitcoin t is

create.davidgomadza7628102bitcoin.start

you can simply say i will create value in the future so subscribe today then get value in the future but also promise to pay us 1 to US$8 per bitcoin we subscribe and now if you ask .ya for extra decrees but in bitcoin he will issue you then start as with decrees if we are to ask what can be createbitcoin7628102 then this is the answer it is bitcoin in real life but the create code one meaning safe and linked to each individual and one that will last forever considering our longevity currently at 3800 3800 3800 3800 3800 3800 3800 3800 3800 3800 3800 3800 3800 3800 3800 3800 3800 3800 3800 3800 3800 3800 3800 3800 3800 3800 3800 3800 3800 3800 3800 3800 3800 3800 3800 3800 3800 all to power 78902867890(power 28789028678902838690284890789028 67890) if we ask what can be create bitcoin then this is the answer we can make it more subtitle to changes in that the more we give at first the higher the value the more we restrict in the future the higher the value if we ask we can add things that can make createbitcoin rise in value these are our parameters we can give out all as createbitcoin decrees meaning just promise to create value without the need to pay upfront for those who believe in us we can as well tell what is to be by looking at current then use all information to predict changes and ours might end up on top after all ours is better

in several ways
1 its linked to life
2 it can go up or down
3 it can be predicted in prices
4 it is what life must be at the end but only in our system linked to longevity
5 it is the best value for your money for early adopters
6 it asks you what can be of createbitcoin and you
7 it tells you when to buy and when to sell
8 it asks you what you can spend and calculates returns
9 it tells you your profit and loss over time so you can adjust things
10 ignores pressures from others but remains uncontrolled by humans but only by market forces
if we are to start then these are the starting values 789890 for creator davidgomadza
sales 28387628983860
miscellaneous 278389
that means if we are to match bitcoin then the above values should remain the same any changes affect everything since we can ask for comparisons to get our true value hence if we ask now on day of creation of createbitcoin by davidgomadza then this is the value of all our bitcoin at start US$38678902867890 meaning that we can easily increase value as longago increase hence something easily achievable now what are our starting values these are
capital 0
createbitcoin for creator:davidgomadza 789890
sales(to sale) 28387628983860
miscellaneous 278389
now the true value will end at
US$28983867890284890 in 2030
why this is because that is the highest compound longago anything creator or human can achieve then death after this number has been reached but can be changed by an act of genius
visit www.twofuure.world/createbitcoin and also www.createbitcoin.world
if we are to start straight away then we can write the creators createbitcoin through a simple create code

create.ask.
create.ask.davidgomadza.createbitcoin.davidgomadza.789890createbitcoin.create.askya.ya

US$38678902867890 this is the current value but we can write this amount as the startup current quantity by removing the US$ leaving 38678902867890 that means we can now simply say:
ask.ya.create.createbitcoindecrees.start.davidgomadza38678902867890.create.askya.ya
approved total issued today
38678902867890createitcoindecrees.start
create.ask.davidgomadza.createbitcoindecrees.davidgomadza.789890createbitcoin.create.askya.ya

FOR MORE INFORMATION VISIT
www.twofuure.world/createbitcoin
and also

www.createbitcoin.world

ABOUT DAVID GOMADZA

Visit www.twofuture.world

www.createbitcoin.world

MONEY PAPER IN CREATE CODE

create.   Start
value2386
operation2739
surfacetension8928
evaporation2386
assortment28286
refinement2126
assortmentwithotherthingsofvalue232829
associatedpress23289ablueprint2928
afinelinebetweenvalueandnotvalues2286018
attachment23286
achievement386
asertion26183819
astortous39386
attire2329
atore2129
aoteret2129
aostero2924
aostert8234
auertert2876
aostere2386
amtnop2398
aoaer2386
aoet2729
aoaetct2873
agertes2389

aoetera2386982818
gaetotero286898

COINS IN CREATE CODE

create.   .start
aser26898
asert26898
asett28981
asserttt28916
assertto29138

DECREEIT

What could be decreeit that cant be money then this is the answer decreeit cant be paper money according to the definition as these are just paper promises to deliver value but if you create a current made decreeit then all your decrees becomes the most valuable above bitcoin that means if you say swap decrees for papernotes without the papernotes that makes your decrees paper money in overnight because all will search for your money to keep their wealth afloat but if you don't print the money then the decrees dies too an alternative is to intoduce a digital current that is called decreeit with total value of 89000000000 and say 1 is 75million

Ask.davidgomadza.earthvalue.start
US$876890 trillion

Visit www.twofuture.world

Createbitcoin CBTC Whitepaper

www.ingramcontent.com/pod-product-compliance
Lightning Source LLC
Chambersburg PA
CBHW031522210526
45464CB00007B/3010